Includes a CD of full performance and accompaniment tracks

Boy's Songs From MUSICALS

· COMPILED BY LOUISE LERCH ·

ISBN 978-1-4234-2988-3

HAL•LEONARD®
CORPORATION
7777 W. BLUEMOUND RD. P.O. BOX 13819 MILWAUKEE, WI 53213

Visit Hal Leonard Online at
www.halleonard.com

SINGERS:

Anthony Colangelo

appeared in the Broadway revival of *NINE*, and Madison Square Garden's *A CHRISTMAS CAROL*. He is featured on many recordings and television commercials and appeared on *BLUES CLUES*.

Noah Galvin

is currently appearing in Cirque de Soleil's *WINTUK*. He just completed the workshop of the Broadway revival of *BYE BYE BIRDIE*, and has appeared on numerous recordings.

Sky Jarrett

appeared in the Metropolitan Opera production of *PARSIFAL*. He also appeared on Broadway in *A CHRISTMAS CAROL* and *DR. SEUSS' HOW THE GRINCH STOLE CHRISTMAS!*

Daniel Marconi

appeared at the Paper Mill Playhouse in *A WONDERFUL LIFE* and has been featured in *NEW VOICES*.

PIANIST:

Lawrence Yurman

played and conducted the Broadway productions of *GREY GARDENS*, *SIDE SHOW*, *THOROUGHLY MODERN MILLIE* and *LES MISÉRABLES*. He is an active New York vocal coach and accompanist.

TABLE OF CONTENTS

Singers on the CD:
Anthony Colangelo (track 7), **Noah Galvin** (tracks 1-3, 8), **Sky Jarrett** (tracks 4, 9, 10),
Daniel Marconi (tracks 5, 6)

Piano:
Lawrence Yurman

Piano and Vocal Tracks recorded at: P.P.I. Recording, Inc., New York City
Tracks Engineered by Chip M. Fabrizi
Piano and Vocal Tracks produced by Michael Dansicker

CATCH A FALLING STAR

from *Forever Plaid*

Words and Music by Paul Vance
and Lee Pockriss

6

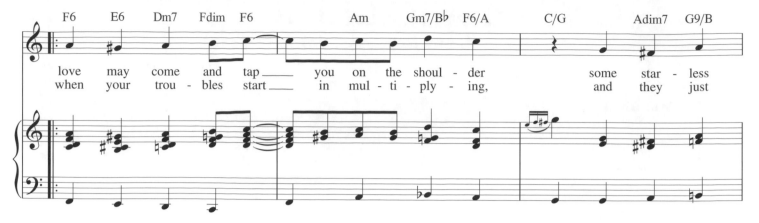

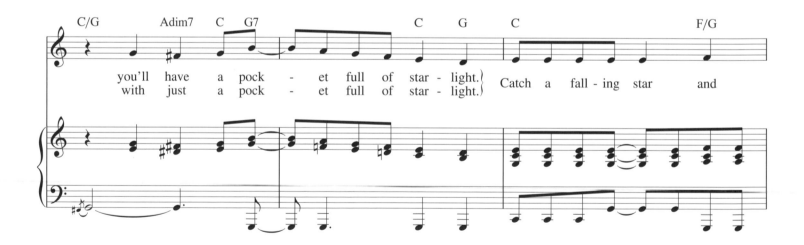

Catch a fall-ing star and put it in your pock – et. Save it for a rain – y

day._____ For day.

Save it for a rain – y day. Save it for a rain – y

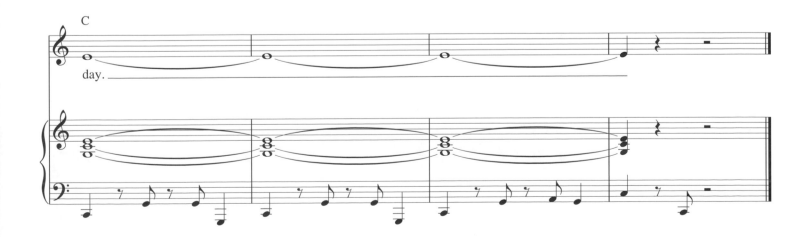

day._____

CASEY JUNIOR
from Walt Disney's *Dumbo*

Words by Ned Washington
Music by Frank Churchill

9

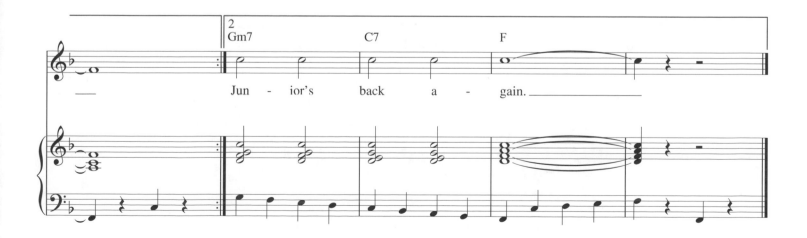

I NEED TO KNOW

from Walt Disney's *Tarzan*

Words and Music by
PHIL COLLINS

Moderate Ballad

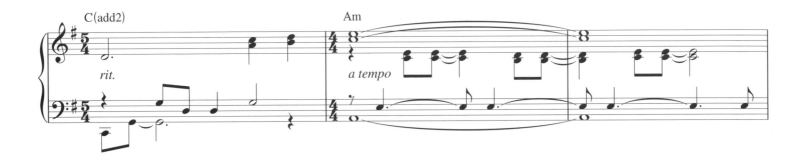

YOUNG TARZAN:

Will some-one tell me where

I be-long, ___ where I ___ should go? ___

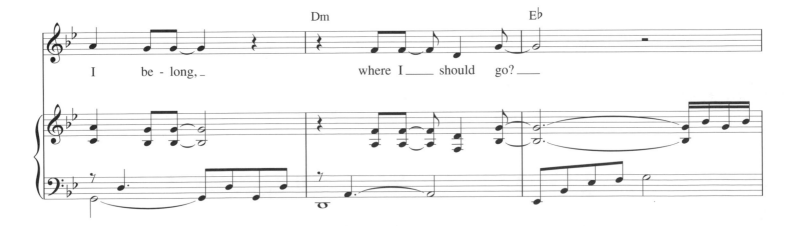

Can some-one tell me where I'm go - ing wrong?_ I need_ to know.

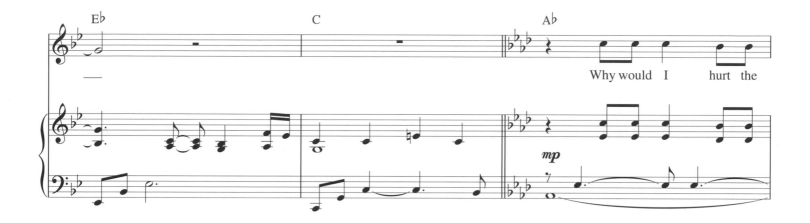

— Why would I hurt the

ones I love?_ Why would I hurt you?__

If I can't be what he wants of me,__ what am I to do?_

12

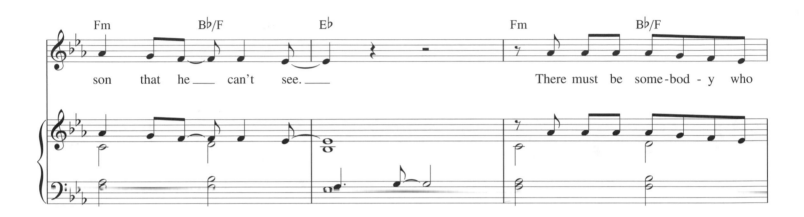

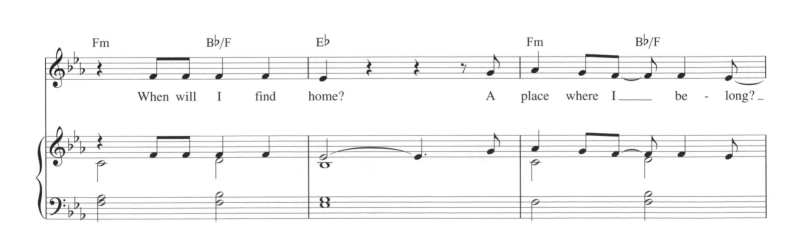

Sure - ly there must be more ___ like ___ me ___ out ___

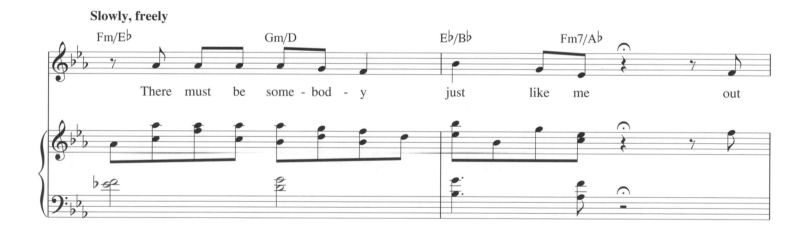

there some - where. _____

Slowly, freely

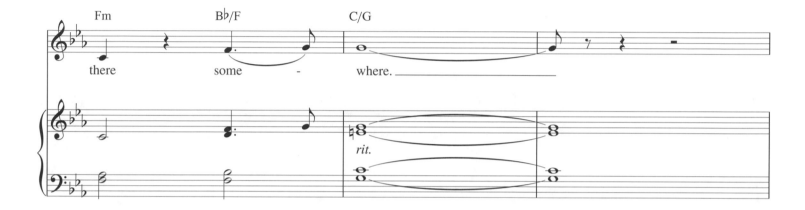

There must be some - bod - y just like me out

there...

I'M LATE
from Walt Disney's *Alice in Wonderland*

Words by Bob Hilliard
Music by Sammy Fain

whis-kers took me too much time to shave. I run and then I hop, hop, hop; I

wish that I could fly. There's dan - ger if I dare to stop and

here's the rea - son why (you see) I'm o - ver - due; I'm in a rab - bit

stew. Can't e - ven say good - bye, hel - lo, I'm late, I'm late, I'm late.

LET'S GO FLY A KITE
from Walt Disney's *Mary Poppins*

Words and Music by Richard M. Sherman
and Robert B. Sherman

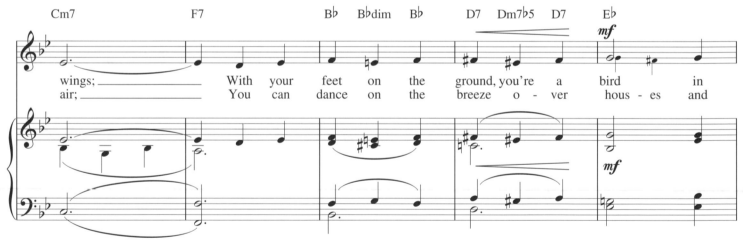

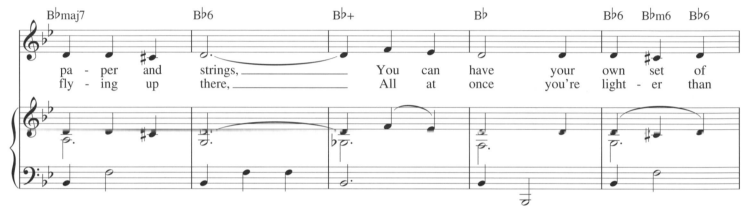

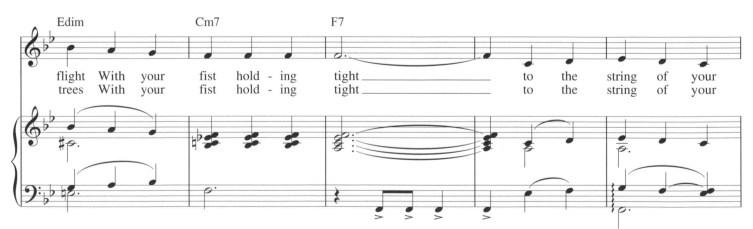

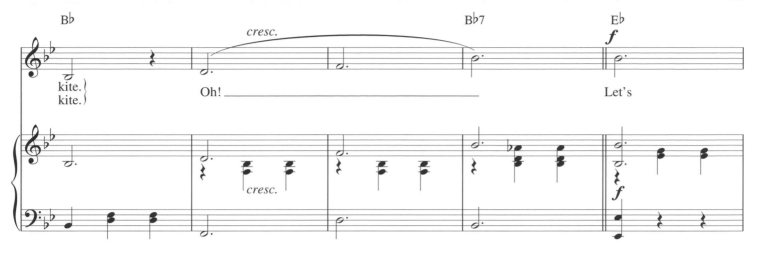

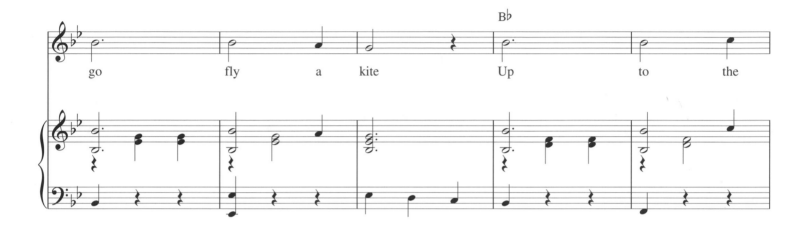

Up through the at - mos - phere, Up

where the air is clear. Oh, let's

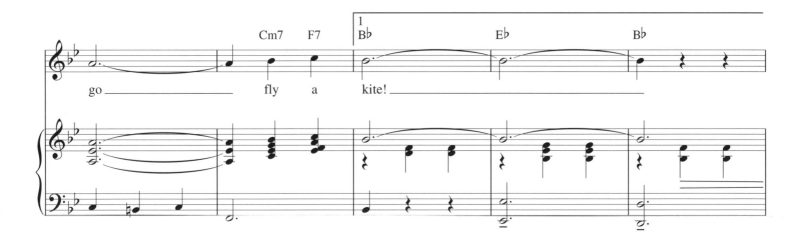

go _____ fly a kite! _____

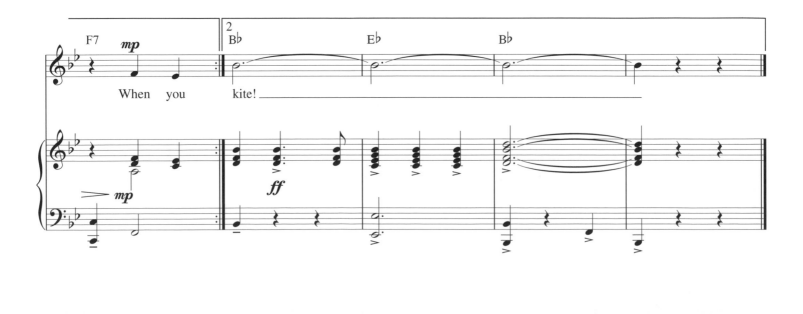

When you kite! _____

NEVER SMILE AT A CROCODILE

from Walt Disney's *Peter Pan*

Words by Jack Lawrence
Music by Frank Churchill

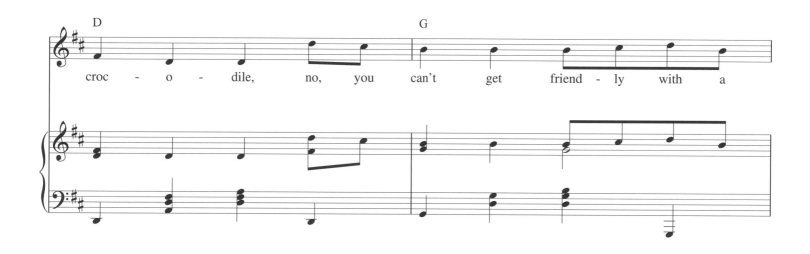

20

ag - in - ing how well you'd fit with - in his skin.

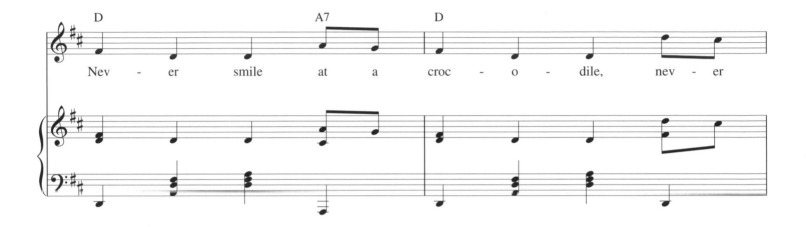

Nev - er smile at a croc - o - dile, nev - er

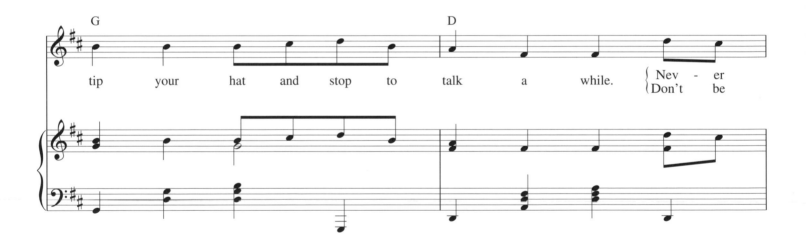

tip your hat and stop to talk a while. { Nev - er
{ Don't be

run, walk a - way, say "Good - night" not "Good - day!" } Clear the
rude, nev - er mock, throw a kill, not a rock. }

To Coda ⊕

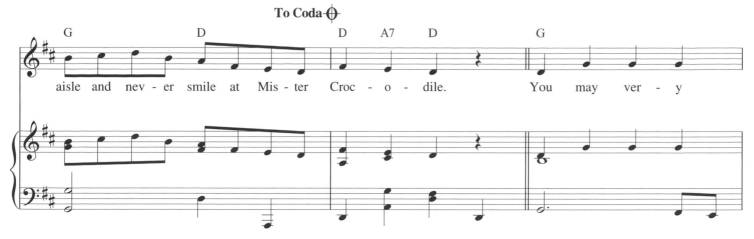

aisle and nev - er smile at Mis - ter Croc - o - dile. You may ver - y

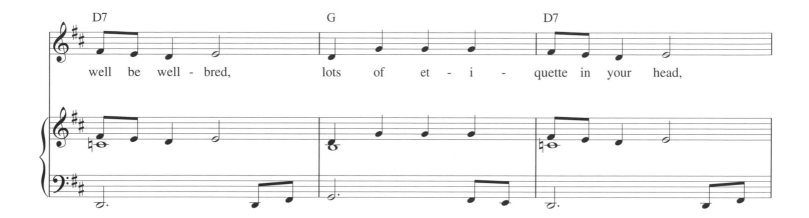

well be well - bred, lots of et - i - quette in your head,

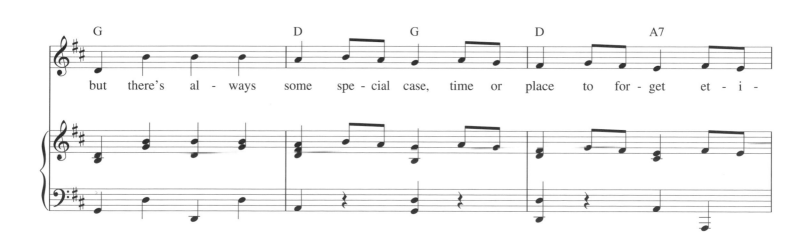

but there's al - ways some spe - cial case, time or place to for - get et - i -

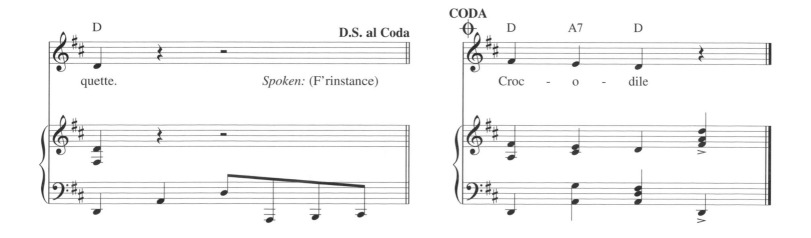

quette. *Spoken:* (F'rinstance)

D.S. al Coda

CODA ⊕

Croc - o - dile

PRINCE ALI
from Walt Disney's *Aladdin*

Lyrics by Howard Ashman
Music by Alan Menken

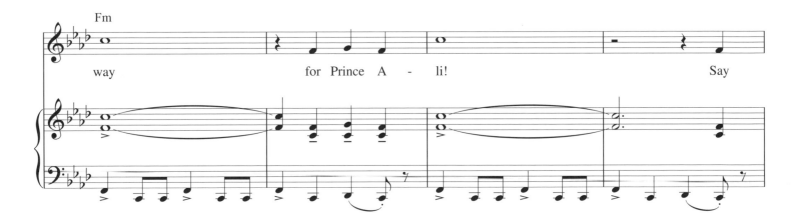

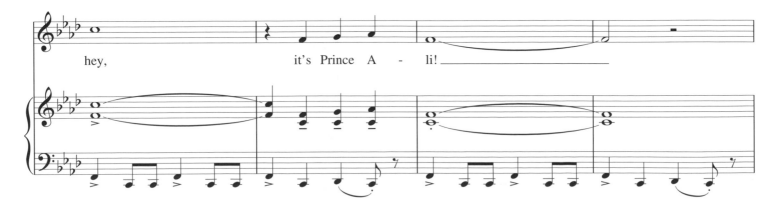

Hey! Clear the way in the ol' ba - zaar! Hey you! Let us through! It's a

bright new star! Oh come! Be the first on your block to meet his

eye! _____ Make way, here he comes, ring bells, bang the drums! Are

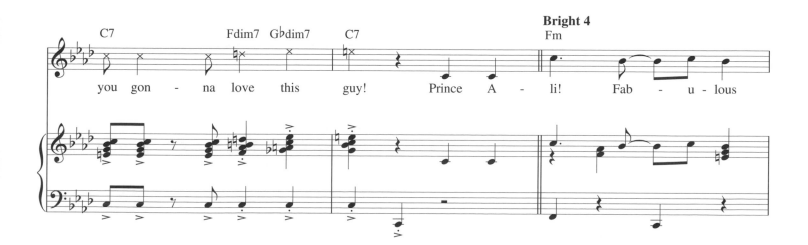

you gon - na love this guy! Prince A - li! Fab - u - lous

24

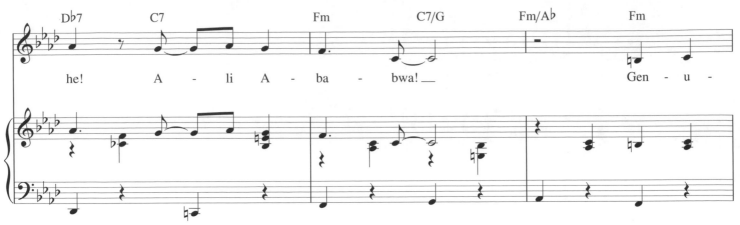

he! A - li A - ba - bwa! ___ Gen - u -

flect! Show _ some re - spect! Down _ on one knee! ___ Now

try your best __ to stay calm. Brush up your Sun - day sa -

laam. Then come and meet __ his spec - tac - u - lar co - ter -

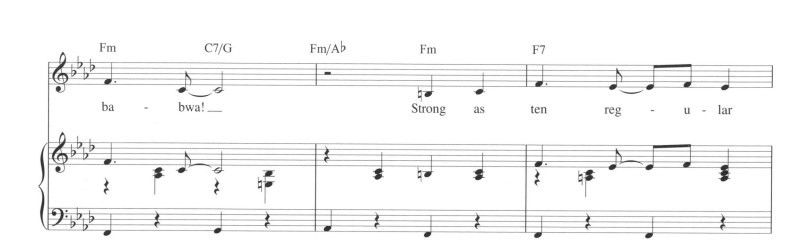

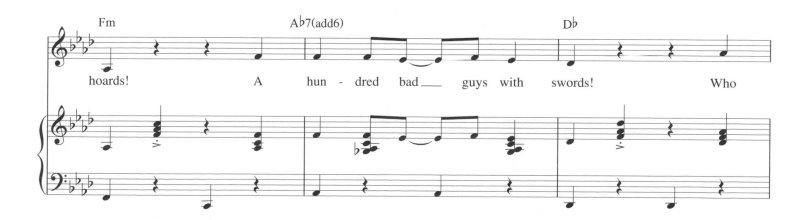

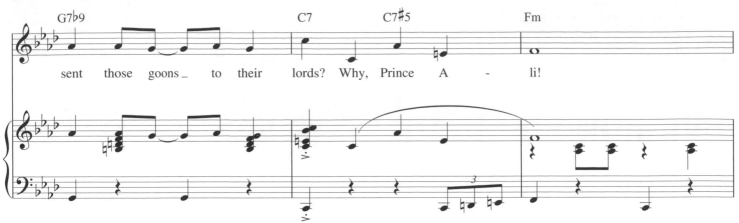

sent those goons _ to their lords? Why, Prince A - li!

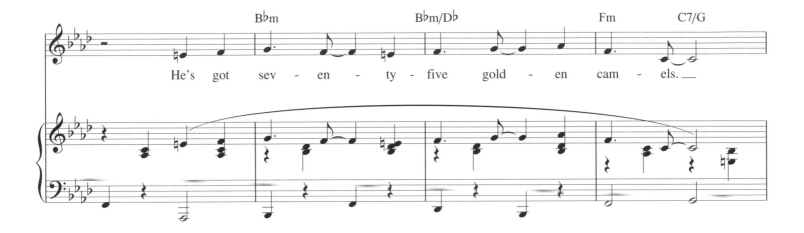

He's got sev - en - ty - five gold - en cam - els. __

Pur - ple pea - cocks? _ He's got fif - ty - three.

When it comes to __ ex - o - tic __ type mam - mals, _

Has he got a zoo? I'm tell-ing you, it's a

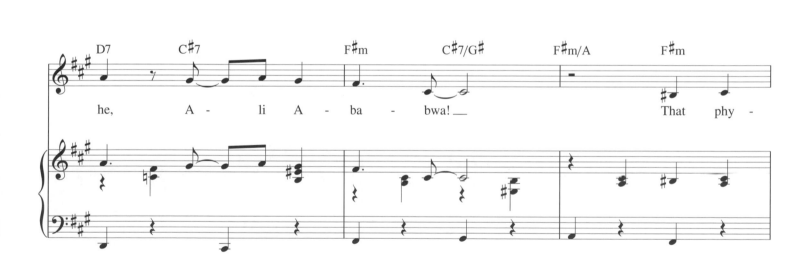

world class me-na-ge-rie! Prince A - li! Hand-some is

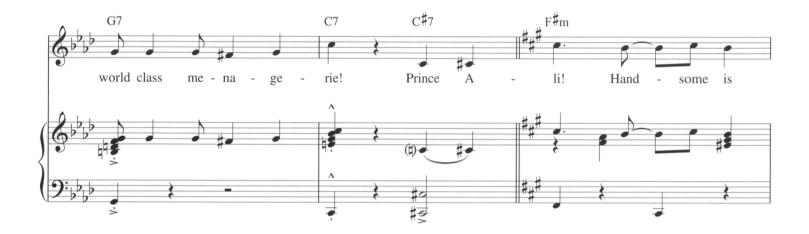

he, A - li A - ba - bwa! __ That phy-

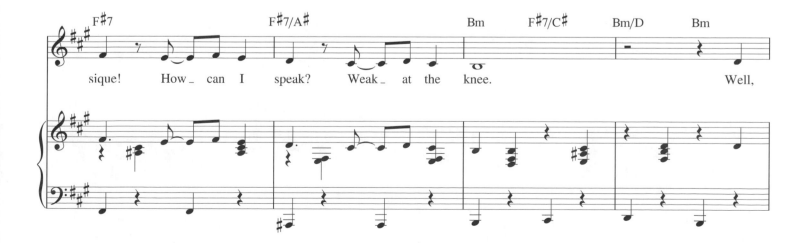

sique! How __ can I speak? Weak __ at the knee. Well,

28

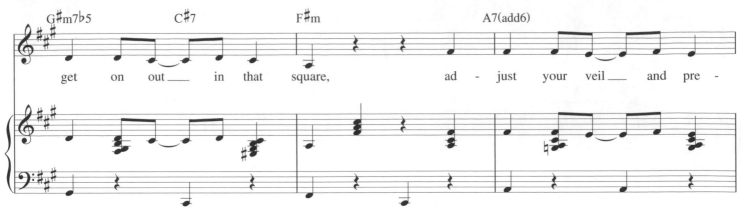

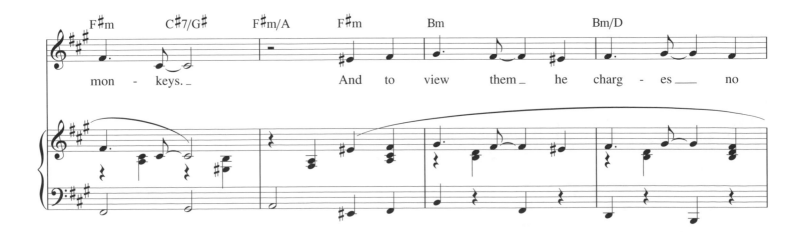

fee.   He's got slaves, he's __ got ser - vants __ and

flunk - ies __ proud to work __ for him, bow to his whim, love

serv-ing him, they're just lous-y with loy - al - ty to A - li!

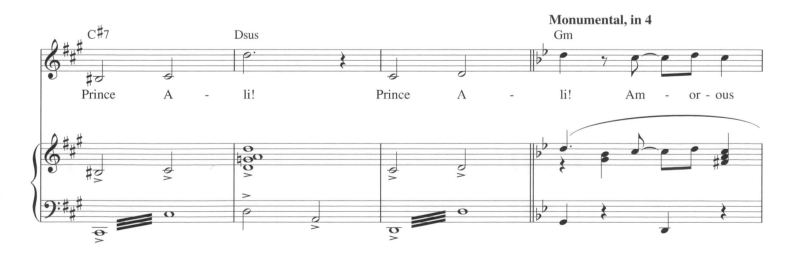

Monumental, in 4

Prince A - li!   Prince A - li!   Am - or - ous

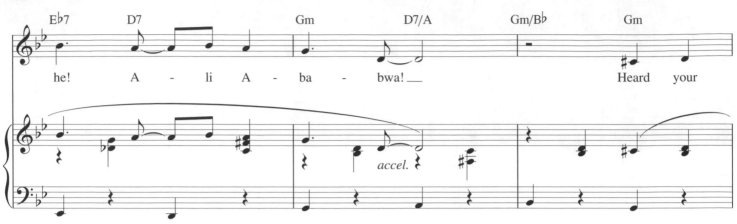

he! A - li A - ba - bwa! __ Heard your

prin - cess __ was a sight love - ly to see! And

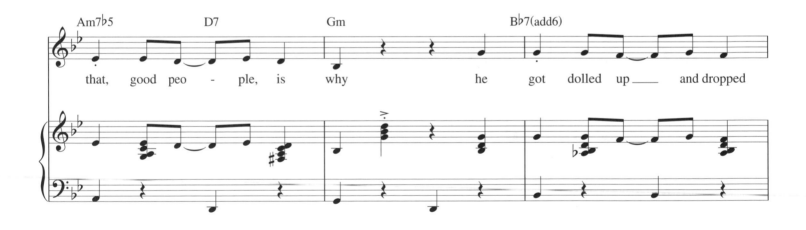

that, good peo - ple, is why he got dolled up ___ and dropped

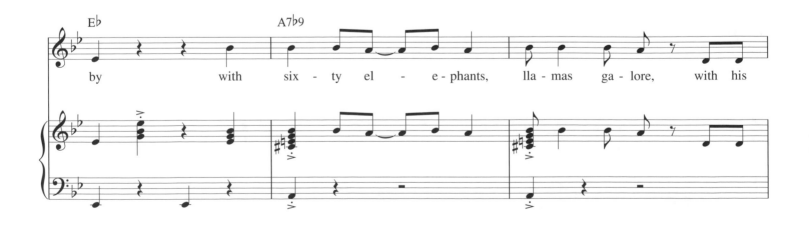

by with six - ty el - e - phants, lla - mas ga - lore, with his

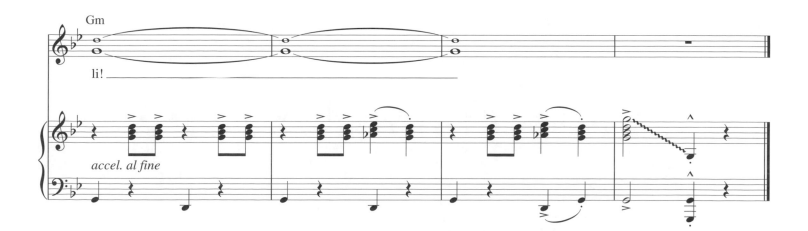

THE UNBIRTHDAY SONG
from Walt Disney's *Alice in Wonderland*

Words and Music by Mack David,
Al Hoffman and Jerry Livingston

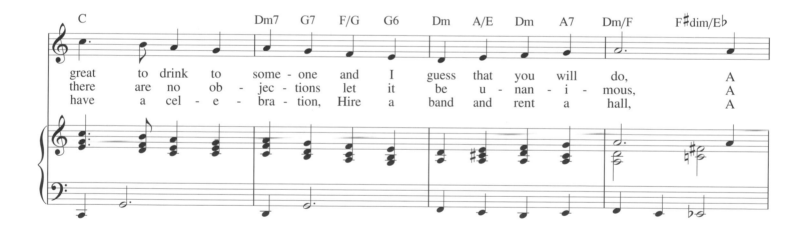

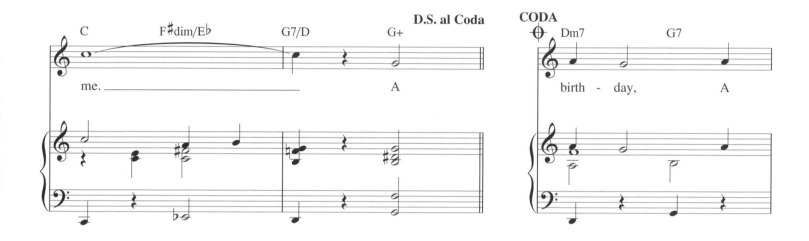

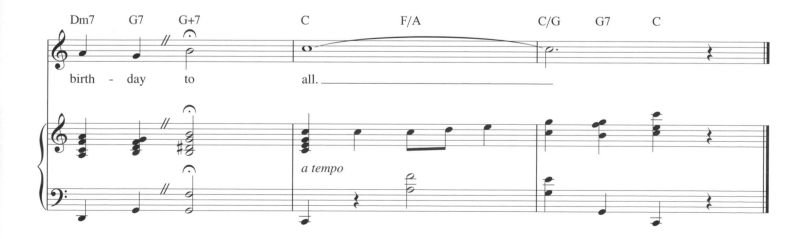

THE WONDERFUL THING
ABOUT TIGGERS

from Walt Disney's *The Many Adventures of Winnie the Pooh*

Words and Music by Richard M. Sherman
and Robert B. Sherman

1. The (3.) won-der-ful thing a-bout tig - gers ___ is tig-gers are won-der-ful
2. won-der-ful thing a-bout tig - gers ___ is tig-gers are won-der-ful

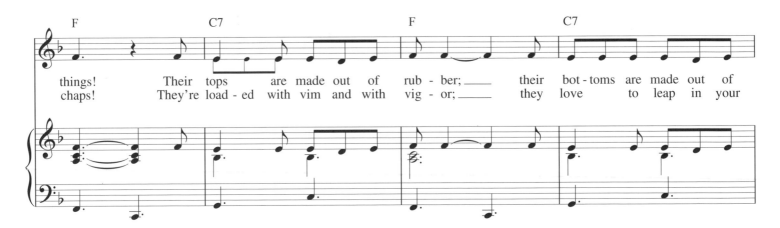

things!   Their tops   are made out of   rub - ber; ___ their bot - toms are made out of
chaps!   They're load - ed   with vim and with   vig - or; ___ they   love   to leap in your

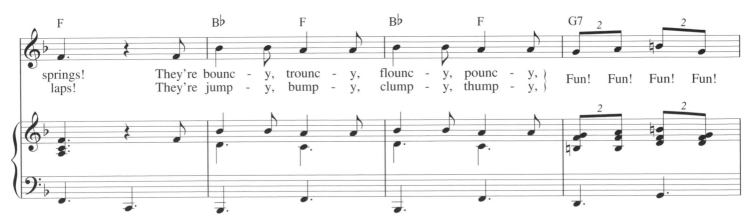

springs!   They're bounc - y, trounc - y, flounc - y, pounc - y,   } Fun! Fun! Fun! Fun!
laps!   They're jump - y, bump - y, clump - y, thump - y,   }

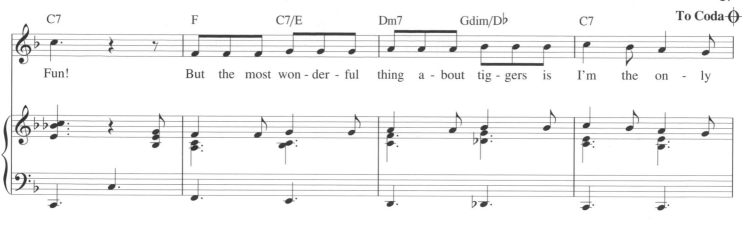

Fun! But the most won-der-ful thing a-bout tig-gers is I'm the on-ly

one! Oh, the one! Tig-gers are cud-dl-y fel-las._____

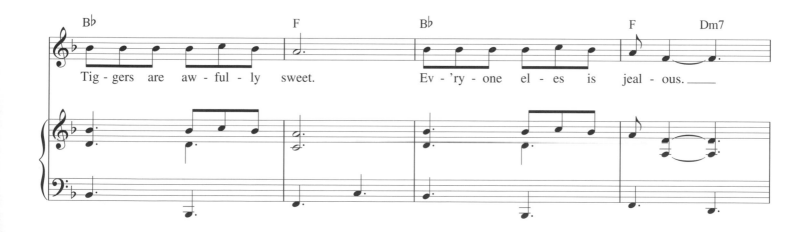

Tig-gers are aw-ful-ly sweet. Ev-'ry-one el-es is jeal-ous._____

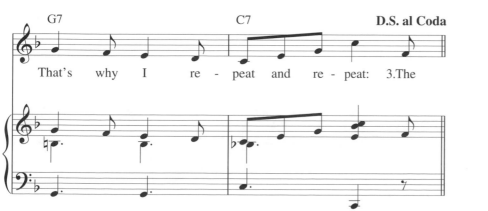

That's why I re-peat and re-peat: 3.The

one!

THE WELLS FARGO WAGON

from Meredith Willson's *The Music Man*

By Meredith Willson

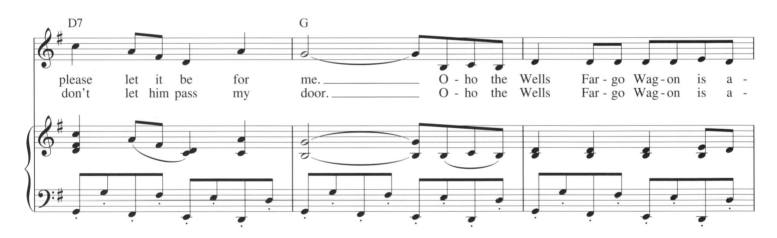

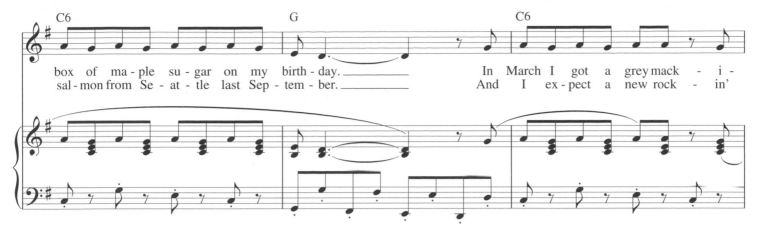

box of ma-ple su-gar on my birth-day._____ In March I got a grey mack-i-
sal-mon from Se-at-tle last Sep-tem-ber._____ And I ex-pect a new rock-in'

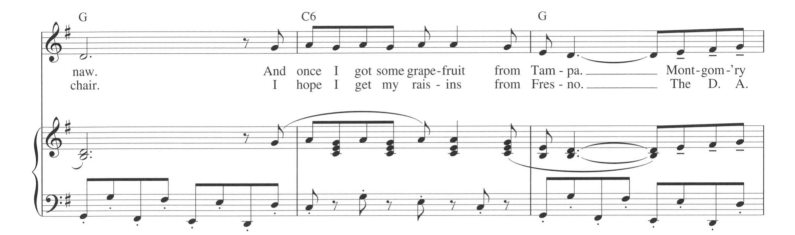

naw. And once I got some grape-fruit from Tam-pa._____ Mont-gom-'ry
chair. I hope I get my rais-ins from Fres-no._____ The D. A.

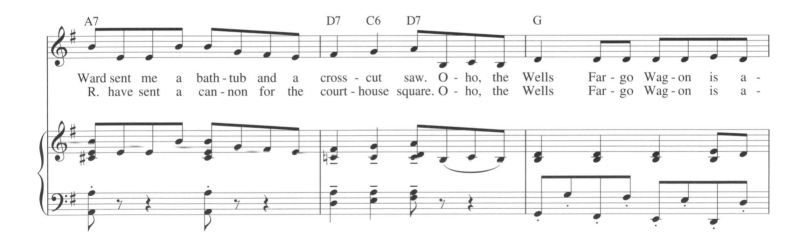

Ward sent me a bath-tub and a cross-cut saw. O-ho, the Wells Far-go Wag-on is a-
R. have sent a can-non for the court-house square. O-ho, the Wells Far-go Wag-on is a-

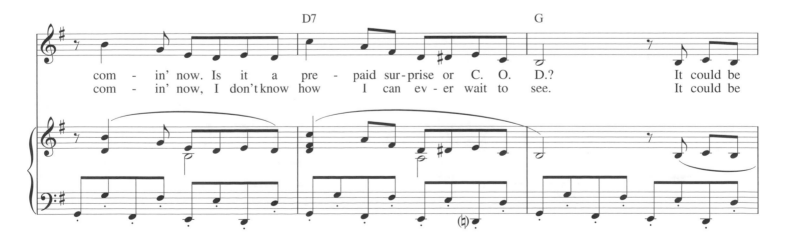

com-in' now. Is it a pre-paid sur-prise or C. O. D.? It could be
com-in' now, I don't know how I can ev-er wait to see. It could be

cur - tains, or dish - es, or a dou - ble boil - er, Or it could be _____ some-thin'
some-thin' from some-one who is no re - la - tion, but it

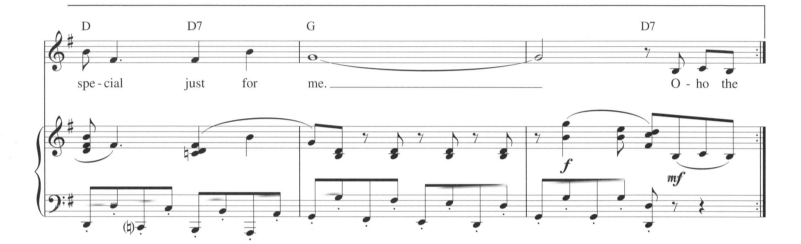

spe - cial just for me. _____ O - ho the

could be _____ some-thin' spe - cial _____

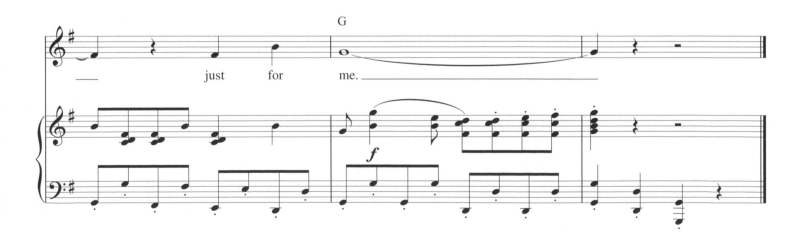

just for me. _____